The Medicine That Burns

The Medicine That Burns
© 2021 by Molly S. Hillery
www.mollyhillery.com

Cover art by Francisca Mandiola
Author photo by Sandy Grigsby at Brio Five

IBSN-13: 978-0-9987729-1-2

Trigger Warnings

This book contains content relating to certain topics that may be sensitive to readers. Please exercise self-care before and after reading. If content in this collection upsets you, please reach out to someone to process. Triggers can be our teachers, if we allow them to be.

infidelity and divorce
(p. 13-45)

mental illness and suicidality
(p. 29, 46-48, 56-57, 101, 107-111, 146, 190-191)

eating disorders
(p. 49-54, 61-72)

self-harm
(p. 85-87, 90, 102, 105)

addiction
(p. 29, 39, 92-94, 186-187)

sexual assault/abuse related imagery
(p. 61, 80-96, 123)

Dear Reader,

This book did not come from beauty.

It came from nights plastered to the bathroom floor and tear-soaked car seats. It came from fighting for control and being so tired that control ceased to have meaning. It came from terror and loss and clean slates and building myself back up from zero again and again. It came from knees-hugging, bottle-clutching, secret desperate struggles that few know of. It came from attempts to cope imperfectly, restlessly, and impatiently, over and over. It came from dark neighborhood walks, vowing to quit therapy every other month, and grief so powerful I thought I would never make it out alive; grief so crushing it took my breath away.

I know what dying feels like.

The death of a former self. She was backed into a corner with all roads leading to exit. Answer the call to live a life rooted in the present, or die repeating the past like it's Groundhog's day.

I am as stubborn as they come. What once was a personality quirk became my Achille's heel. I would not heal your way. I would do it *My Way*. And so I tried, without success, until my fourth and final relapse into my eating disorder became the momentum I needed to catapult me into a life I did not ask for, but would never abandon. A pendulum cannot swing forward without going backwards first.

I insisted on healing the clean, tidy way. The *therapy once a week, yes I am doing what I need to, yes I am eating, no I am not harming myself*, box-checking, go-through-the-motions healing.

But healing is a mess.

When would I arrive at the destination? When am I off the road of healing and onto the next highway of life? Self-destruction is simple; it was embracing the softness of life that pained me the most. The tenderness tortured me more than any of the burns, the cuts, or the self-indulgence of self-injury. I realize now that the anguish I endured was just further research for the role of "healed."

Some days I had to tell myself that it was better to grieve a love than to never have loved at all. In my case, the loss of love was weaker than the blows of feeling a life, unlived. A life permeated by an undying thirst for things to be different, with a mind that told me not to drink.

I did not choose healing. It chose me.

With honesty and love,
Molly

Contents

(2,309 days)

With You

How painful it is
to have a partner
that sees right through you
You are no more
than a glass door,
shielding them from freedom
And as they stare beyond
the wall you represent
wishing to be relinquished,
you wonder why
they are keeping you
closed and untouched
all on their own

I used to be afraid
of you dying one day
and leaving me
to fend for myself
Over time,
the obsession lessened
almost into apathy
I promise it is not
that I wanted you to die
I just held less fear
of what my life would look like
without you in it

Slowly,
we became passing ships
Prisoners, co-existing
in the same cell
without windows
Oh,
What have we done to each other?

All at once,
we are living in a house on fire
Standing before you,
I call to you for help
My extinguisher,
let us escape this fiery prison
that has engulfed us so fast
I pray you reach me in time,
pulling me to safety
where we recover from this mess
But the embers have you captivated
and you simply stand back,
marveling at the flames
You do not hear me in the chaos and
my desperate pleas
are silent screams
falling upon deaf ears
and losing themselves in the heat
You devise an escape plan
to suffocate the blaze
and I am lost alone in the inferno,
wondering who tried to smother it
when it was insignificant
and who ignited it,
making it incapable of survival

Ground Zero

I fiddle with my wedding ring as they excitedly ask me what it is like to be married. They want the juicy details, as if it is school-yard gossip, or some type of elderly wisdom. I sense they want me to tell them hopeful things; things to keep their pupils twinkling with hope.

"What is the best thing about being married?"

It occurs to me that the word "love" does not come to mind and I feel damaged. My answer falls flat on my audience and I fumble. I try to recover and humor their optimism for a moment.

"…But you love him, right?"

They do not know what a complicated question this is; how loaded the word "love" is for someone like me. I do not blame my nightly companions— they are so young.

My smile fades and I stare off into the distance for a little while. And as I enjoy the rest of my night in the company of lively, unjaded young women…

I have no idea that you are with someone else.

Without You

When you left,
the noise stopped
Not the physical noise,
but the space that was filled
with all the words
you never said.

-Silent House

Day 1

I wonder where you would be without me today, and I wonder where you will be later without me. I think about the things that were once "ours," returning to "yours" and "mine." There is more brokenness to this process than just you and I and there is more division to be done than just our material possessions.

I think about the home we purchased a mere nine months ago, and I curse us for our terrible timing in all of this. If these walls could speak, they would tell you stories of arguments without words and crippling fear. They are filled with that bad kind of nostalgia; the kind that seems to envelop every empty space and coat your lungs with melancholy. Like you are breathing in sadness. I can't fathom living out my days in this vessel of painful memories.

In my heart I know that the pain of feeling like the only half fighting for us is the reason I am so sure of the answer today. The burden of that pain has finally lifted, yet the pain of the realization that I carried that weight alone and unrequited still lays heavy on my heart. I imagine the day I move out— such a painfully public ceremony and display of our end. I picture seeing your family for the final time and wonder if perhaps, it was last Sunday.

Maybe it is better this way.

Day 3

I need to channel my feelings into something, *anything,* so I start to clean. I oddly wonder if divorce sales exist, like estate sales do.

Self-blame wraps its arms around me and promises relief. Within minutes, the tightness of its grip is suffocating.

Our walls look bare now.

Day 5

The dog is whining incessantly, wondering where you are. She perks her ears up every time she hears a loud engine like yours drive by.

I keep asking myself how I am going to get through each day. Here presents the very real madness in being exhausted from measuring my life in small chunks of survivable time. During my drive home, I remember that I am going home to nothing and for the first time in all of this, I do not feel relief in your absence, nor anger in your betrayal. *I miss you.* I miss how things used to be, although now I can barely salvage memories of it being pleasant. The trauma of the last two years has invaded my mind to where nothing exists in that space but heartache.

We used to be happy.

It is in this moment that I wonder if I will ever be okay again.

Day 10

I met with an attorney today. I know he has no real stake in my personal life, yet seeing his "Dad" mug and freshly polished wedding ring, I couldn't help but feel his judgment for computing the fiscal value of my marriage to be next to nothing. Our relationship is bankrupt in more ways than one, and I begin to cry in his office. The grief continues to pour out of me in unabashed ways.

I am a shell of my former self.

Day 12

My newfound superpower is silencing a room. No one seems to know what to say to me. My mind subconsciously places people into two categories: those that understand my pain, and those that do not. Friends with seemingly successful relationships become a "them."

And I?

A "me."

My aloneness feels like a gaping chasm.

Day 14

I arrive at the coffee shop early to avoid searching the crowd, but mainly to avoid being left with the awkward question of whether to smile or acknowledge you when you show up. When you sit down, I am distracted by your bright appearance, your calm and peaceful demeanor, and how I don't even know who you are anymore. Maybe I never did.

~~~~~~~~

I drive with panicked desperation and make it home just in time to unleash my rage within a contained environment. I scream into pillows and chase my sadness with shots of rum. I feel my life unraveling, and the sudden change in you is an unexpected punch to the gut. You are not as sad as I am and that somehow makes me feel as if I am losing. I feel the pain of what our relationship became and the damage I allowed it to cause me, even through glasses of booze.

The weight of the cemetery of my relationships, my inability to become close to people, and everything I could have done better begins to gnaw at me. Within minutes, it is feasting on my flesh.

I want to die.

It crosses my mind once, twice, and before long it is all I can think about in my drunken haze. My self-destruction is only halted by waves of uncontrollable vomiting. In the darkest passages of my brain, I find an image of you, twisting my intestines while I heave. And with every bit that swirls down the drain, retching…

I picture me getting rid of a little more you.

Day 16

Our relationship is dead, yet the ghost of our lost love is alive and well. There is nowhere to visit for closure in this aftermath; no bare ground to lay flowers at your feet.

Years later we may talk, and my memories will not match who you are in that moment. We will be strangers.

Where is our grave?

Day 18

I forced myself to meet with friends tonight. After several minutes of well-intentioned conversations about "us," I grabbed my empty martini glass, excused myself, and smashed it in the alley behind the bar.

It was all I could do to keep from crying right there on the smoke deck.

Day 19

Walking on the treadmill at the gym, I recognize a familiar figure. An old friend that spent time with us in our early days. I haven't seen her in almost seven years. She threw the party several weeks ago.

The party.

After several minutes, I strangely find myself glaring at the back of her head. I increase my walking speed as my cheeks become flushed. Soon, I feel pressure as heavy as a hydraulic press crushing my lungs. The weight crashes down on me as I fit the jagged puzzles pieces together in my mind. My heart pounds as if trying to escape my chest cavity. My stomach drops the way it does on a roller coaster.

It is my body's reaction that suggests it, and the smirk on her face when I approach that confirms it.

It's *her*.

I run to the women's room and open my locker with shaky hands, the code, our wedding day (6/20). I gather my belongings and pause to catch what little breath I have left. I feel I am going to explode into a million fiery pieces right there on the gym floor. My insides are like thousands of rubber balls being thrown full speed into a tiny, locked closet. There is nowhere to discharge this energy. My body becomes a prison for this fury.

I rush to my car and speed frantically to a park I rarely go to in good spirits. I sprint through the woods as fast as my legs will move, until my breathlessness feels within my control. I sprint until I don't feel real.

I am not in control anymore.

Day 63

I am a sad person. I spend most of my time alone at my sad, under-resourced job. I eat my sad microwaved meals in my big, sad house built for more than just me.

I feel as though my friends invite me to things because clearly, I am sad. Sometimes all I can do is sit and be sad around them.

I am so sad I don't know what to do with myself. I don't know how to relax. I don't watch TV, read, or keep up with people as much as I should. Every ounce of downtime I get, I work. I clean. I do everything in my power to pretend the sadness is not there.

I used to be someone else. I used to meet society's expectations of "happy." I used to be able to accept my sadness, because at least I was a part of a pair. *At least I wasn't alone.*

The truth is that I have been alone for a long time. Sometimes love is not enough. I am not going to receive answers as to what was so wrong with me in those final days that you couldn't be the person you are now when we were together. And right now, to me, that is the saddest part of all.

Day 93

I am leaving behind everything I know. Near a decade of existence, transformed in a matter of days. Years of assets, money, and memories with this person must now be categorized, separated, and stowed away for the sake of healing and "moving on."

The despair comes for me in the evenings when the house is hauntingly quiet and still. This is when the ghosts of our failed marriage look me straight in the eye and dare me to fall apart. This is when my mind screams at me the most.

I must concede to the fact that I will not feel settled or stable for a long time. I know I cannot just snap my fingers and be okay, and that I cannot rush the healing or magically flash forward a year from now. I know that massive amounts of change are in my near future, yet I do not know how any of it will turn out. It is not an adventure to me.

It is a nightmare.

Day 114

Tomorrow I will be moving out of the place I call home. A place I assumed I would be rooted in for years, perhaps even decades. I will live in this vast, echoey space full of cardboard boxes and old memories until I am allowed to take refuge elsewhere; until my new home officially stops being "someone else's." The emptiness of the walls and closets where my things once were serve as a cruel reminder of what could have been. My thoughts carry me to the day I was ecstatic to finally own my own home. How naïve I was then.

The house did not represent a fresh, new start— it symbolized an untimely demise; the rapid deterioration and eventual death of my marriage. It was a year of trauma and isolation and fear; of "what if" and "could be" and "why."

I purchased new items I will need to signify my "new beginning." Material possessions don't bring me much comfort, but I find solace in knowing I won't constantly be reminded of the things we once shared.

Mom joins me on the deck this morning while I smoke. I turn to her and see tears in her eyes.

"Why are you crying?" I ask, shocked at this sudden shift in emotion.

"...Life just sucks sometimes, doesn't it?"

This feels more like a rhetorical question to me. All I can do is retort that this is a little heavy for a Sunday morning, but only because I fear I will melt into a puddle right there in front of her. There is no time for that now.

"You're right, that is kind of heavy," she agrees.

This satisfies us both in the moment.

Month 7 Without You

It is a rainy October night. I have cleaned all night and completed my usual rituals, but it isn't keeping the rumination at bay. Thoughts of you creep in as I scour the bathroom floor.

Are you happy?
Why aren't I?
I miss you.

Scrubbing the bathtub cannot rid me of these nagging thoughts.

This life is permanent.

I want you to come over and watch stupid TV with me, like we did when we were young and in love. I have spent so long remembering the bad things— the memories I clutch with vigorous desperation, to keep me from wanting, from missing, and to sustain detachment from "us." For once, I do not want to self-destruct. I want to pour my heart out to you. To this page. To anyone who will listen. *Why us, like this?* How do I grieve someone who is still alive and a life that never came to be?

I have nightmares of you with other women

I know. Of the alcohol, the fights, the fear. The feeling of not being in control together.

Being angry is too hard, too painful, and too much. The physical manifestation of my solitude feels too difficult to bear in this moment, but I must hold onto the conviction that we are not supposed to walk through the rest of this life together.

So this is the "after," a world where you and I no longer exist. A parallel universe, where you replace me with a new her. We have gone on living despite it all.

I thought you were my ticket out of a town filled with bad men…but that is only for fairy tales.

Sick

You

I made you the villain
in order to survive.
You scared me.
You violated my boundaries.
You stopped caring.

I hid from the truth:

I scare me.
I violate my boundaries.
I care too much.

I ran from what I feared all along:

I am the villain.
I am to blame.
I wreck things.

I have no answers,
only more questions.
I do not deserve to move on.
I wish things were different.

Me

Welcome Home

I see photos of people I used to call friends celebrating your new phase of singledom with you. A "Welcome Home" party has been created, in the house we all used to spend time in together.

Did they see signs I once existed there?
Did they think of me?
Do they know what happened?

Sitting in my apartment alone, I finally succumb to the belief that I truly was poison to you. I was a cinder block, tied to your ankles. Without me, you are free.

The heaviness of my heart is enough to drown me.

Just Like You

You have some of my mail. I prefer you leave it on the doorstep of the house, but I come inside at your insistence.

You have built the bonfire pit you always wanted.

You have two new roommates who never seem to leave the house unless you do.

You have six family-sized bags of chips on the table. As I gaze at them, you say with a grin, "We had a party over the weekend."

I should be happy for you, but resentment and pain surround me. I don't tell you that I am alone all the time, that I can't sleep, or that I am not eating. I take the mail and leave with a half-hearted smile.

Anything to show that I am just like you.

A Dull Ache

My therapist asks how I am surviving. I shrug. Life is surviving. I tell her that helplessness becomes a dull ache, no longer an urgent wound. You learn to live with the pain.

She is quiet for a moment, examining my blank stare, contemplative.

"Yeah, that's it," she says.

A dull ache.

I feel myself being pulled into
the darkness but I do not
know if I am strong
enough to keep
it from
swallowing
me
alive.

-Drowning

I feel a void within my body.
Is it possible
to feel something that
technically is not there?

-Empty

I am frozen in time
and once again, I am starving
The hunger,
gnarls in the depths of my belly
helping me forget
The hunger,
to be anyone other than me
I am alone.
I am alone.
I am alone.

Safe//Unsafe

The bare bones
of Maslow's hierarchy
I am an animal in the wild
The intricacies of life melt away
as I focus on my next meal
and whether it is
safe or unsafe
It is a strange experience
to hear another voice in your head
and know it is not yours
It is cruel and nasty,
but you are frozen in its clutches
I feel my eating disorder's claws
around my throat
and somehow I know,
it has come to rescue me again

Are safety and control synonymous?

A Stranger

There is something oddly comforting
about the inability
to recognize myself in the mirror
I am flesh and bone
Smallness, nothing more
A person unrecognizable and
I inhabit a body
that no one has ever hurt before

Living Contradictions

I need food	yet detest and avoid it
I am constantly isolated	yet never alone
I want more out of life	but am too terrified to break free
I despise the rules and rituals	but cannot stop abiding by them
I think it keeps me safe	but it puts my life at risk
I feel in control	but am the definition of out of control

I have moments of what I think
is clarity
I don't feel normal
I'm not healthy, I say
I want so desperately to stop
these compulsive, humiliating,
and at times disgusting behaviors
A constant push-pull
Some days I want to scream,
I am suffering!
I am dying!
I am not okay!

Yet to do so
would hand over the reins of control
which my mind has told me,
is death in itself
I am physically and mentally sick
but somehow, I have told myself
that I need to be sicker
in order to get well

R-E-L-A-X

My coworkers and I sit at our desks this morning, discussing how time at work has been limited lately. I mention that I took my laptop home and worked because I was anxious about meeting deadlines. One of them snapped back,

"You know, you really just need to relax."

I wince. I want to explain why I am so high-strung all the time, but all I can muster is,

"I know, I'm sorry."

Pathetic. I choke back the tears for a few minutes, then cry quietly at my desk after she leaves.

I dream.

I dream of running away— from myself, my life, this job, and this city.

I dream of telling my therapist the truth. Of standing up for myself at work. Of telling my loved ones what I am really thinking or feeling aloud, *just once.*

I dream of what it would feel like to feel worthy of recovery. To live without compulsions or rituals. To live without "must" and "have to."

I dream of a life with less fear and mental illness. A life where I hear the voices in my mind and notice the circumstances in my life trying to beat me down and for once, *I do not listen.* I do not base my worth off of what happens to me.

I dream of a life where I thrive, rather than a life where I survive.

My illnesses pull me back to reality and remind me that none of these things are possible. Powerlessness is a state of being. I drink and smoke and compulsively clean any space I inhabit. I ritualize and count and create idiotic rules to live by that I somehow believe will keep me safe. I run to my eating disorder because I cannot stand to be in my own company and because even if it means I put up with an abusive, invisible partner, at least I am not alone.

I feel trapped in a world so tiny I can barely breathe, but the world out there? It is vast and frightening and has hurt me terribly. I wake up every day convincing myself that this life, of smallness and self-destruction and "safety," is somehow better. I slog through my days counting the minutes until it is over while simultaneously calculating the number of days I believe I will be able to carry on like this.

When will I finally break?

I tell myself that tomorrow will be different, but it never is. Another day comes and goes and nothing changes because nothing changes.

So for now I do what I do to get me through. And I keep dreaming.

Take a Sip

Mother's Day

My parents visit me this Mother's Day. They drive three hours to see me and tomorrow, they will be driving me to treatment again.

I push away memories of past Mother's Days I have ruined— like the night I never came home after Prom. The images are as clear as yesterday. I stood feet away from the boy who raped me, feigning a smile while our parents proudly clicked their cameras and gave us commands to "Say cheese!" My date left me crying on the dance floor. I was an angry girl; a sloppy drunk playing the role of self-assured. I disappeared, neglected my phone, and made my parents worry simply because I could. They found me in the early hours of the morning, hugging a toilet at a party house. I ordered them to leave, but that plan was foiled. I sat in church the next day, Mother's Day, hungover. A shroud of shame around me. I couldn't explain the pain back then.

I feel that same shawl of humiliation wrapped around me this Sunday, twelve long years later. Still sick. Still struggling.

They go out for dinner alone because I can't bear the thought of eating at a restaurant and not ritualizing at home, as I have been doing every night for the past six months. I eat my small meal and make them a decadent dessert for when they come home. I fight hard to join them and compromise with half of a cup of diet ice cream for myself.

It is the best I can do in the moment.

Ground Zero Part II

I know my mind is ill, but that doesn't change my behavior. I just want to make it there safely.

Mom debates whether she should stay with me while I finish my paperwork. Usually I shove them out the door, or, during the times I was well enough to transport myself, called them when I arrived. This trip feels different. I am too tired to make a decision, too drained to play independent.

She leaves. I wait until they bring me onto the locked unit to slump to the floor and cry.

Day 3

I feel like a tiger pacing its cage. I run my fingers over my sacral bones for comfort. I trace along the veins of my forearm as if they are part of a sacred treasure map. I place my hand on my hip several times to check the amount of steps and calories I have burned on my pedometer, failing to remember that I left it at home.

Relinquishing control to others while you are unwell is a learned practice. This phantom pedometer pain is just one of the many uncomfortable feelings I will soon force myself to accept. No addictions to hide behind. No unhealthy coping to distract. I am stripped bare of those things here.

I am naked.

Sandwiches

It was "surprise" sandwich day earlier this week on the unit. The spontaneity of it was too much for my brain to process. I couldn't finish. I had a "perfect" streak of completing meals and I ruined it. I ended up slipping a kitchen knife up my sleeve to self-harm with later.

On Thursday, we were given sandwiches again. I was having a difficult day coping and ended up sprinting out of the dining room, down the solitary hallway to my room. I slammed the door and proceeded to have a violent tantrum. I howled, punched the bed with rage, and hit myself as hard as I could. I dug my nails into my arms, banged my fists against my temples, and screamed over and over that nothing is fair. All seemingly over a sandwich.

But that's the ironic thing about eating disorders: it isn't really about the food.

It never was.

This body does not belong to me.
This body is not mine.
This body is not home.

Day 24

It is difficult to get well for a subjective idea
or fantasy of what life will look like after "ill."
Sometimes I feel I am not strong enough to
recover solely on blind faith.

Continually making the choice to get better
is committing to the possibility that I may
experience profound disappointment, loss,
and grief even when things are going well,
with no behaviors to soften the blow.

I am terrified to process the events that acted
as a catalyst for this relapse.

Days 50-80

This is the part where all I write about is food. How much I obsess about it, how often I talk about it, and how many tears I cry about it. Food I have to eat, food I have to drink in supplement form, and food I refuse to eat and then pay the consequences for.

This is where I fight everyone designated to help me, because I am too tired to fight the part of my brain that wants me dead. As I regain my faculties with continued nutrition, the memories resurface. The rage, the loneliness, the pain. I cope the only way I know how. I elope, I self-harm, I lie. I gain trust to have small amounts of time away from the unit and end up in the emergency room with alcohol poisoning, needing stitches. It is a story I have lived a thousand times, though I never plan it to be this way.

Your illness screams because it is dying.

It saved me after heartbreak, but I know that in these moments, it is killing me.

A to B

One day this will all be worth it
I will confidently proclaim
I am glad I went through that
but knowing you are in-between
point A and B
on the timeline of your life
does not make *now*
any less painful
Everything happens
in its own time
which is the saddest
and most relieving part of all

Divine Intervention

I can only describe some of the events I have endured in treatment as divine intervention.

To conquer the make-up of my physiology and make choices that my illnesses would never allow me to, is a spiritual experience. This is when I grasp hold of parts I never knew existed. This is when I choose to listen to the tiniest ounce of bravery, courage, or logic that I have left.

This is when the magic happens.

The Voice

I cannot physically force my feet to take me to lunch. I want to, so badly.

I want to eat.

I want to think clearer. I want to be myself again. But I am overpowered. The voice of my eating disorder hisses that I am nothing without it. It cackles in that shrill way, because it knows it is winning. I am tortured and have taken up residence in the calm-down room. I choke out the words,

"I want to eat!"

I writhe in pain. In this moment I feel I have lost something entirely crucial to my survival: control. My thoughts are so deafening it hurts.

Staff assure me that yes, the thoughts are loud, but <u>they will go away</u>. I can't break free of the thoughts until I properly nourish myself. I have told myself I cannot eat because the thoughts are too loud, but the thoughts will *never* become quiet if I do not eat. How do you consume the one thing your brain has convinced you is poison? The tug of war in my mind is nothing short of agonizing.

I walk into lunch twenty minutes late. It is a meal I do not prefer. It is not the perfect lunch, but *it is just food.* Medicine. One step closer to clearer thinking. One step closer to being free from the voice, once and for all.

I AM CAPABLE

1.
of getting out of bed
of getting dressed
of taking my medication

2.
of showing up
of participating in therapy
of being honest

3.
of self-awareness
of doing things that soothe me
of planning for the future

Some days will be 1's
Some days will be 3's
It does not matter where I fall
because at the end of the day,
I am always capable.

I am willing to occupy this body in exchange for what recovery brings.

Motivation for Recovery

To stop the cycle of relapse
To stop serving self-destruction
To be free from the rules in my head
To be present in my life
To form true connections
To give myself a chance
To make family and friends proud
To find inner peace
To make a difference somehow
To not waste life hating myself
To find meaning and joy
To learn how to cope with pain and
suffering
To be able to show up for others

Because I am curious
Because what do I have to lose?
Because I can always go back to being
miserable.

One Moment at a Time

This life is mine again. Done are the structured schedules, meal plans, groups, and appointments. *I am going home.*

The apartment looks just like I left it.
"See you soon," I hug Mom and Dad goodbye. "Drive safe."

They leave me and the dog in silence. The depressing fluorescent light in the kitchen flickers, then dims. I glance at the empty fridge, whirring. The food scale I left by the toaster confronts me. I couldn't bear to throw it away before I left. The old ritual of throwing out the "tools" calls to me, but in this moment, I am tired. I feel loneliness creep up and I fight it, fearful that urges will wash over me like a tidal wave before fully consuming me.

What now? Watch TV on my depressing couch and pretend the past seven months never happened?

I assure myself that there will be plenty of time for plans. I just have to get used to this new life…

one moment at a time.

Swallow it Down

In 2017 I wrote, *"If I distance myself from the pain long enough to realize that these thoughts are the result of my past and not my present, I can still continue to grow."*

Since then, I have learned more about what it means to be traumatized. Distancing myself from the pain is not the problem. It never was.

In order to truly grow, I need to know my pain. I need to speak to it like an old, cherished friend. I need to understand why it is still here after all these years. It is not enough to be merely surviving in gray. I want to live life in full color.

Whether I can handle the confrontation of haunting memories so distinctly imprinted on my mind, still remains unknown.

I am willing to try.

March 31st, 2006

I hand Mom the letter and race upstairs to my room. My heart pounds. If I close my eyes, I can almost hear the blood rushing to my face; an imaginary seashell cradling my ears. I see red beneath my eyelids and I patiently wait like a lamb to the slaughter.

Knock. Knock.

My blood pressure soars. I don't want to unlock my door and face them, but I am not an adult yet and have no choice. This seems to be a theme in my life lately: no choice.

I am not prepared for the barrage of questions, of the gentle, quiet concern so sickening it makes my stomach churn. I don't know quite what I expected, as there is no rulebook on divulging your assault to your parents at the insistence of your school administration.

Mom kneels at the end of my bed. Dad is standing in my doorway. He cannot bear to look at me. He does not say a word. I am met urgency, a silent operation to uncover facts.

I don't believe that you were not drinking.

Unexpected, calm disdain.

I gave you trust back after your suspension. I thought you had learned your lesson.

I feel nauseous. Acid rises in my throat as I willingly endure the worst type of emotional punishment a child experiences from their parents: disappointment. Possibly anger. At who, I am unsure. I presume it is me.

Dad exits, leaving me for the interrogation. I outline an imaginary figure on my jeans. I bite my lip and hold my breath. My cheeks burn with shame as I avert my eyes.

After the third question about my rapist's genitals, I fly away to somewhere else. If you apply pressure to me, I'd turn to dust and scatter away. I don't fight to stay. I hastily tell her what I need to, in order to make this disappear. I desperately want life to return to normal.

But they will never be normal again.

[I forgive you].
[I forgive you].
[I forgive you].

We were young girls
turned into
knowing women
and the world
taught us
to be silent.

His teeth, knock against mine
like various colors
of bar table pool balls
It is his turn to break
His appetite, voracious
like this is the last meal
he will ever eat
It is his turn to feast
His desire, insatiable
like nothing can replenish
his emptiness
It is his turn to restock

This is what it is like
to be played
This is what it is like
to be hunted
This is what it is like
to be emptied

The Beasts Inside

They are the bitter nothings
in my ear
The malicious whispers
only I hear
They tell me stories of things
I dare not speak aloud
And in this silence I feel shame
I am covered in a shroud of

Violence.
The kind you don't know,
until you do
Abuse lives here
My very own Medusa,
touching parts that turn to stone
the kind too heavy to carry
but oh,
I carry.
I carry.
I carry.
These free-floating stones
splinter my insides from time to time
A hole that is not filled
because they filled mine
when I did not ask
And now this galaxy of blackness,
this cavernous abyss,
this vortex of ghosts I used to know,
is what they call home.

Brokenness.
The kind you cannot describe,
and you cannot try to mend
Rage lives here
My very own Godzilla,
destroys anything in its path
I have felt this broken
for as long as memories exist
and with nowhere to go
but out,
I break.
I break.
I break.
broken mirrors
broken hands
broken plates
broken hearts
broken in
broken down
I want to break them all
just like they broke me.

Filth.
The kind you cannot rid yourself of,
and that no amount of bathing will clean
Shame lives here
My very own vermin,
polluting me from the inside out
I have been dirty
for as long as I have been woman

dirty hair
dirty knees
dirty shirt
dirty please
all the stains are washed away
but the memories.

Mutilation.
The kind you cannot understand
and is so intensely private,
it is almost holy
Self-hatred lives here
My very own Vampire,
siphons me so often
that sometimes
I even scare myself
Wounds coat these arms,
these legs,
these chains,
that keep me tethered to the hate
I carve you out of me
the most artistic way I know
And as I gather the tissues
soaked in red,
I place them on every part
of my body because
this is what it feels like
to have you inside of me.

And as my wounds weep,
so do I.

How much pain until I am valid?

Sometimes therapy feels like
an exorcism
Sometimes it feels like
they gave me demons
to carry in the pit
of my chest forever

The Worst Kind of Movies

A series, of flashes
Vomiting, stumbling
Your breath on my neck
My hands, clawing, clutching
I am overpowered
I am choking, stifled
You are winning and
I, becoming the very worst thing:
your victim.

A collage, of memories
The white-tile ceiling
Your rhythmic inhales and exhales
The vibration of the highway
I hurl objects into the abyss
I shatter mirrors with my fists
I self-inflict lacerations and
I, becoming the very worst thing:
out of control.

A montage, of images
My defensive arm raised
Cold tears streaming down my face
You slamming the car door
I scream into pillows
I scream into the void
I scream at people I wish were you and
I, becoming the very worst thing:
a monster.

My mind replays these scenes
possessed by repulsive themes
I am tied to a chair,
too frozen to glance away
And on my worst days
these flashes,
these memories,
these montages of images…

are the worst kind of movies.

My Memories of You

The brilliance of the closeness
The nights we spent alone
The youth we kept, so dear
Our future so unknown
Tears in your eyes, our wedding day
when you looked at only me
Rescuing our own sweet dog
and our house, our family to be
With this we were ecstatic
Our future, we could see
Not long after I took your name
I no longer felt so free
and now we are

Underwater, feeling darkness
blocking sunlight we let inside
We close the blinds
We shut our eyes
Our sicknesses we hide
The indulgence and the relapse
that turn friendliness to fear
The unpredictability
the "Grab me another beer."
The separation that we forced
to keep us safe from "us"
I find you unconscious one day
and you, I no longer trust
We've been through this all before
when at first, the problem was me

With you, it's new
and I don't know what to do
when sober you cannot be
I won't forget the scenes I've seen
of you, helpless under its spell
And you're not "you,"
you're angry too
in these destructive fights, you yell
The doorknob forcefully turns
You shout and scream "Let's talk!"
You never go to bed angry
but if so, why can't you knock?
Where are your fists
are they gripping my wrists
and forcing a kiss, once more
The intimacy we coerce
to fix the source
of our problems
behind the bedroom door

I push you away
I can't meet your eyes
and your glance fades away again
I blame myself
because on my shelf
of baggage of course, is men

We play a game
of who self-destructs first
We don't know the score
or care anymore

We waste our days
our own separate ways
until it becomes too much to bear,
and my memories of you
turn gruesome too
and enabler a label, I will not wear

I loved you once
I can't right now
but I don't know how to leave
I'm frozen inside
I just want to hide
and safety with you, I grieve

Until one day
you've fixed it your way
and you've been with someone else
With this act, I decide
I cannot abide
by a marriage with no pulse
You're sober now
and joyful too
A woman, you've found is new
and I'm over here
remembering the years
of the memories I had
with you.

The Darkness

The truth is that no matter what, I will always live with ghosts. I have seen the darkness of humanity. I have seen the edge of death. I have seen angry, drunk men as scared little boys. It is something no words can fix, no gentle embraces will heal, and no half-hearted apologies will rectify. At the end of the day, I went through my trauma alone and scared. And there will always be a part of me that lives alone, and scared. Whose entire world is darkness. This part is preserved in time and will not accept my adult condolences.

People want pain to be clean, tidy. Healing to be courageous, visionary. Not messy, not out of the box. People benefit from trauma being neat and orderly. They benefit from our silence and they benefit from our strength when we wear the title of "Survivor."

Part of me will always be drawn to the gruesome parts of life, the need to look into the eyes of the ignorant and shout, "This is what the world is truly like!" *Why can't you see it like I do?* Why can't you touch parts of other people's pain?

Suddenly relationships feel pointless, work trivial, and all you can think about is how broken you are and how sad life is. You are angry when people tell you to think positive. *Have you touched evil like I have?* Have you seen the worst, most vulnerable parts of people acting their pain out on you and lived to tell the tale? Instead you paint a smile, make small talk, and swallow it down like a watermelon seed in summer.

We are the gravediggers, knowing how to bury our pain and make it more palatable to the outside world. We are the ones that stifle ourselves so you won't be burdened. When we speak of our pain, we are strange. We are wet blankets. We are negative forces.

I try to move on, to release it, and to focus on the positive. The more time passes, the more burdened I feel.

I start to live parts of my life in the shadows.

Spit it Out

Hope is a Precipice

You've worked so hard,
the journey so long
They didn't doubt you,
but they were wrong
to think you're capable
for you know,
it takes more than
just work to grow
There is willingness and honesty,
but most of all hope
It is much more crucial
than tools to cope
But hope is a tricky thing for you
If they knew your story,
they would agree too
That when you're high,
there's far to fall
Hope is a precipice, after all

There is freedom and beauty
at the top,
but when you slip
it's hard to stop
The landslides more dramatic
than before
Each time you drop,
you keep the score
And stow the reasons
to stay sick away

The devil you know,
a more comfortable stay
With each descent,
it becomes harder to recover
You fear the worst,
that you'll soon discover
You weren't really meant
to experience good things
and all of the joy
a healthy life brings
And you don't really have
another loss in you,
so keeping things safe
is how you continue
For when you're high,
there's far to fall
Hope is a precipice, after all

PTSD

Sometimes it feels like I am living with a tumor inside my mind. Specialized treatment shrinks it sometimes, and symptoms become less present, but I can relapse at any time.

Different parts of the tumor are like boulders: weighted placements inside my brain that never leave. Lodged deep in-between the synapses, they are lessons that traumatized parts of me keep locked away to avoid the same mistakes that left me hurting.

The tumor affects the way I think and act and live. To remove it would change my personality and the way I function in this world.

It could be for the better, but it is a terrifying unknown.

My behavior when I was young was impulsive, self-destructive, and dangerous, but I do miss not caring. It was a state of being, really.

Not Caring. ©

There was something very freeing about not carrying my burdens so heavily. About being completely detached from myself and others, with no regard for the future.

I didn't worry so much.

Supposed To Be

Our bodies,
our relationships,
our words,
will all fail us at one point or another
How can I live a functional life
if I crumble
with every perceived deviation
from the script of *supposed to be?*

The Darkness Part II

Who am I without it?
Who will I be when I am healed?
Why am I allowed to move on from
the things that have happened to me?

It is a strange confrontation during self-analysis to admit that there is a part of me that craves the darkness.

It is such an integral part of who I am.

♡

I don't want to do the self-love stuff.

Part of me thinks that therapy will fix me, and logically I know that work also has to be done outside of sessions. Using skills and avoiding harmful habits while the work is being done is important, but certain self-destructive parts just aren't willing to give up their vices yet.

I know I will have to suffer a little longer before I become willing again. Always with this cycle.

It drains me.

Self-Compassion

I kneel in the middle
of the wild forest,
vulnerable
I wait for the wolves
to come feast
on my flesh

Self-forgiveness means
I lose the armor of self-hatred
that shields me from
the carnage of life
For they cannot destroy me,
if I have already
destroyed myself

Loving myself
will make losing myself
so much more painful
Losing myself
has made loving myself
so much harder to comprehend

What it Means

Having a disorder rooted in complex trauma means having such a fragmented sense of self that oftentimes, people cannot define who you really are. It is having a deep knowing of profound loss, while simultaneously being a bewildered, lonely being. It is being in your thirties, but feeling too mature and too naïve at the same time. It is not relating to your peers in their strife because you are only worried about day-to-day survival. It is having the wisdom of an old soul, while still being emotionally frozen in adolescence.

Being triggered means being catapulted into an existence where you are five years old again, hugging your knees, and hiding in the corner of your apartment. It is mornings laid out on the couch because of nightmares, and nights sleeping on the floor like you did when it felt safe. It is seeking comfort wherever you can find it: in weighted blankets, stuffed animals, and even expensive new technology, but certainly never trying to find it in another person again. It is shouldering adult responsibilities, while feeling less capable than the modern adult. It is having a trajectory in life that does not constitute as normal by societal standards. It is shame that you cannot be just that: normal. It is wondering if your life was meant to be this way, or if you chose it to be this way. It is coming to terms with the difficult truth that being traumatized during your prime developmental years means there is a good chance that trauma will try to find you throughout the rest of your life. It is blaming yourself for the helplessness that you feel, but feeling incapable of long-lasting change. It is having a brain that is hardwired to find danger, but being looked upon as weak for having anxiety.

Living with chronic trauma is not for the faint of heart. It is a difficult path to follow and a hard life to live. I know there are healers out there who understand. I know there are people who feel the same way, reading this right now, saying, *"Yeah, I know what that feels like."*

I hope we can find each other.

There is still an ocean inside of me. Asking me to self-regulate when I am triggered is like asking me to swallow vomit; while the acid rises in my throat, I choke the tears back down into the body of water that I am. I can't hold my breath any longer.

Please help me turn the faucet off.

Trauma Therapy is Triage

It is pulling small bits of shrapnel out of my wounds, week after week. To pull it all at once may kill me. I examine the miniscule shards, one by one, and maintain equilibrium until my body adjusts to this new shape of hurt within me. It changes, slowly. It hits parts that hurt more. Sometimes it hits arteries, and I spend the entire week between appointments attempting tourniquets and clotting techniques. Some days I want to rip it out in all of its bloody glory. The urgency to fix it is agonizing at times, but I am told this is the way to do it: slowly and steadily.

With every new trigger, I wake up to a world where something isn't healed; a new wound festering that I cannot ignore any longer. There are days when I pick at wound site just to feel that pain again, to see if it is still there. There are days the hurt seeps out, leaving nothing but underdeveloped pink flesh to protect me. My therapist helps me close the wound temporarily, but some days steri-strips and glue do not equal thread, and it feels like the despair could spill out of me at any second. I try to take care of it, but it is difficult to do between appointments on my own, month after month. Year after year.

I am afraid one day it may just kill me. I ask myself if I can live with this bullet lodged inside me forever. I contemplate if I should stop trying to have a better quality of life, but I have already started the excavation process. It feels too messy now. To stop at this point would be unsafe, it seems. Some days I think to myself:

Even if this does kill me, was I ever really living before?

Caterpillar Soup

I read somewhere that when a caterpillar is completing its metamorphosis, it completely shifts into a pile of goo before becoming a butterfly. It liquifies its old body in order to transform.

If you cut open a chrysalis in the middle of its transformation, the goo will ooze out and the butterfly will never be just that— able to fly. It is kind of horrifying, but miraculous if you think about it.

I think that is maybe what healing feels like.

Caterpillar soup.

Walk Without the Pain

You broke your foot years ago. For whatever reason, it did not heal properly. You thought you were fine. Physical therapy seemed unnecessary. You jumped back into regular activity quickly. You denied its severity and ignored the pain for a little too long. You just wanted to return to normalcy.

Years later, you are suffering the consequences. You have copious amounts of scar tissue and chronic pain. It hurts more at certain times of the year, but those times seem to affect every aspect of your life. You can't run like you used to, but you see others running marathons. You can't wear heels like your friends do, so you wear flats and tell yourself you look fine. You hear other people complaining about being sore after a workout or a long day on their feet, yet you know what it feels like to live in silent agony and discomfort twenty-four hours a day. You swallow your words because it would be rude to compare. You begin to resent others for being able to move about with ease.

After quite some time, you realize you may need professional help. Things are not progressing like you thought they would. You see a specialist and reluctantly let them test your strength with different exercises. You are uncomfortable at first, but tell yourself this will change things. It will be worth it in the end.

Over the years, you see many specialists who promise to help you with your foot. Surgery to dig out the scar tissue. Physical therapy to live with the repercussions. Some odd new technique that promises to solve the problem completely. Some give you medicine for the pain and send you on your way, telling you to manage it the best you can. Some spend too much time making you relieve the details of the original injury, and you become confused. Some of the exercises designed to heal you end up injuring you more. Maybe they misjudged and pushed you into activity too soon. Maybe they thought your abilities were greater than they actually are. You have been faking wellness for so long, you forgot how convincing you can be.

You do not get better. You grow weary. *Why are so many professionals ill-equipped to deal with poorly healed broken bones?* Surely it is not that difficult, if that is what they are trained to do. You grow frustrated and stop trying to heal your foot. You decide to live with the pain. Sure, you manage it a little unconventionally, but they are not the ones with the useless foot. They don't have to learn how to live with the hurt, because their feet work just fine. For a while you consider amputation. Your friends and family are worried at how reckless you sound about it all, failing to understand just how far gone you are.

Along the way, you meet some brilliant and talented professionals who know how to help you with your foot issue, but you have been living with this for so long that you have grown accustomed to the pain. You do not trust them. You have decided that you will never be "just like everybody else." Soon a life without this pain seems foreign…scary even. What would it mean to have a fully functional foot? Will people expect the same things of you again? Your abilities have been dampened for so long.

You know these professionals are sincere and you entertain their notions of full recovery, but you do not fully believe them because of the ones who claimed they could help you and ended up leaving you wounded and more enflamed than before. These new experts are patient. They are kind. They slowly walk you through the process of healing your foot. And sometimes it is so torturous, you want to stop. You push back. You stop making appointments to see them.

What do they know, anyway? Have they ever lived with this pain? It is just going to end up the same as it was before. *"Maybe I like it this way,"* you say. Maybe you don't know if you even care anymore.

You continually find yourself at a fork in the road. Continue the way you've been going, or take a risk and try again. New method. New specialist. New research. More money. Sometimes you hate yourself for defying the only people who seem to be able to help, but you try to tell yourself it is only because you have been let down and hopeless in the past.

It is a long road with countless twists and turns, and at times seems endless. You remain as consistent and vigilant as possible, mirroring the mantras that your specialists repeat back to you when you are doubtful.

And you hold on as long as you can, with hope that maybe someday, with hard work and patience…

you will one day walk without the pain.

Double Dose

The Road to Healing

Some days I ask for guidance
in keeping my eyes on the road
Some days I succumb to the impulse
to jettison into the ditch below
How do I ask these wounded parts
to step away from the wheel?
When their pain isn't in charge
and they truly believe the words
"You are safe now."
I will never be able to leave them
on the side of the highway
They will always find their way back
And though they are too young
to be steering,
they don't trust the adult
that insists it is not their job
to travel down pavement
they shouldn't have been on
in the first place

Her Office

I sit through
what feels like
the most cruel,
fiery death
over and over
I am reduced
to ashes,
week after week

After I am burned
for what feels like
the thousandth time,
I rise.
I blink through tears
and open my eyes
to a new room
in front of me
I spread my amber wings
and reveal myself:
beautiful,
broken,
strong.

I break
and I heal
again and again.

Fearless

She said I was fearless
Where did she go?
I am afraid of her
Of the lion girl made of fire
who flew through finish lines
and stood up to bullies
Who stared down life and said,
"Give me all you've got."
She said I was fearless
Where did she go?
I am afraid for her
Of the girl who shed tears for animals
and people who sat alone at lunch
Who felt so intensely,
the world seemed to stop
when she wept
She said I was fearless
Where did she go?
I am afraid of myself
Of becoming her again
Of being "too much"
Because it seems life has
broken her heart
She learned to be quiet
She learned less is more
She learned if you play with fire,
you will get burned

She said I was fearless
Where did she go?
She is buried deep,
crying out to be heard
She is locked in a cage
within my heart
She is tired of being oppressed
Of this body being a prison,
and not a home
Of this life being carefully controlled
I want that little lion girl to be free
She said I was fearless
Where did she go?
I am her,
and she is me.

Sixteen

Where is the line
between honoring her
and forgetting her?
Her ghostly presence,
always bellowing in the spring
She whispers soft warnings
and blinding rage when I do not heed
I told you to keep me safe
My body, the in-between
Her spirit remains earthbound and
I relive her death
in the quiet moments alone

All I ever wanted
was to vanquish her
and the memories,
but I cannot
Our pain waxes and wanes
with the moon and tides,
year after year
For she is me,
and I am her.

Sometimes I think love
is nothing more
than letting yourself be loved

Mothers & Daughters

I think daughters in my generation
were born to fill holes
in our mothers
Not just empty wombs, but voids
that ached for their own mothers
that yearned for
corrective experiences
that said, *"I will never be like her."*

I think a maternal instinct
and an obsessive need
is one in the same
The chance at a do over,
a retribution,
a reckoning,
A prayer in the bunker of womanhood
A desperate cry to the Universe
that said, *"I will do better."*

I think being alive
is an oath,
a test,
a duty
An experience they never had
A chalice of wishes
to the thirstful flower children
who wanted all the love
this world had to offer

125

A promise to their psyches
that said, *"Make me whole again."*

I think women know how
to break their own hearts
better than anyone in this world
We ignore our own damage
to house another soul,
and expect them not
to be broken too

We felt your pain
Your swallowed feelings
and your fears of inadequacy
Your dreams cast aside to have it
"All American"
We felt it through the tightening
and the hours of darkness
We felt it through the cord
and the milk you bred us
to sustain life on

I think women my age
have strong shoulders
from the albatrosses
our mothers gave us
We carried their feelings
of being unseen,
unloved
Of having too much responsibility
placed on their shoulders

It is something you can't explain
You know down to your bones,
your heart,
your red and white blood cells,
how important you are,
how broken she is,
how much she wished you
had declared her healed
the day you left her
and joined the world

I think little girls
are the most observant creatures
on Earth
I think they see things
we cannot understand or explain
Mothers, we saw the milky figures
of our grandmothers inside of you,
wandering
An offering of outstretched hands
An invitation rarely accepted
A plea often ignored
We are haunted, like you
but we hide it well

I think this is how
it must have always been
Generations of mediums
who carry shared pain
Who relive the traumas of their mothers
with each inhale and exhale

127

they have left in their lifetime
Loyal, rebellious, protective beings
through unspoken promises
and collective wounds
Wild, angry women
Who take their last breath
engulfed in flames
Who light their undergarments on fire
in the streets
Who post naked photos on the internet
and dare to scream
"THIS BODY IS NOT YOURS."

I think this is how
it must always be
Women creating women
to be more broken
and more whole
than ever before
Mighty containers,
that embody so much pain
Bodies that have a deep knowing,
a silent rage running
through their veins

We are conduits
for the oldest of mothers
Who never had them
Who never knew them
Who saw them every day,
yet lived with ghosts

Who survived,
so that we could live
They gave us suffering,
but they also taught us
how to thrive

I think mothers and daughters
are the most special,
fucked up
kind of spiritual
that exists on this planet
I think most of them
would agree, too.

Crybaby Part II

As a child,
hiding away from family
As an adolescent,
curled up in my room
As a teenager,
lying on the bed
As a twenty-something,
with my fiancé beyond
the locked bedroom door
In these tears,
I am always alone.

I am now thirty,
on the bathroom floor
Outstretched palms,
cupping tears of old wounds
Humming a silent battle cry:
Life is brutal

The dog nudges the door open,
bowing her head
A peaceful offering beckons
as I soak her neck with my tears
This being, embodying feelings
I never let myself feel
I swallow the antidote in small doses:
I am never alone.

A Universe exists
where the limits of truth
have no bounds
I live in a knowing Universe
and I tell myself
this is enough
to carry me into the morning

Life is brutal
It doesn't mean anything
if you cry alone for 100 nights
then publish a book
shouting, "*I am healed!*"
We are not meant
to swallow these big feelings
to make others comfortable
We are not meant
to swallow these big feelings
and grieve all by ourselves
Sometimes I think about
the lonely people out there,
making themselves agreeable
and wearing the badge of "strong"
Shrinking their feelings to fit
the big wide world around them
I want to tell them
what I wished I believed
in my own solitude of tears:
You are never alone.

We are all connected
in this honest quest for catharsis,
seasoned with the salt in our sobs
and the wounds in our whimpers
And for this reason we say:
We are never alone.

On the Mend

To be loved is to grieve
when I have told myself
for so long, I am unlovable
I did this to survive
and it is okay to let it go now

I can acknowledge unhelpful thoughts
without acting on them
I can be gentle with myself
when I make mistakes
If life is going well,
it doesn't mean
it will be perfect
If life is difficult,
it doesn't mean
it will stay difficult forever
Rinse, lather, repeat

-Shower Thoughts

I have survived
every emotion
I have ever felt
I almost did not survive
my attempts
at escaping them

I am not ashamed of how I show up when I am struggling.

I can be irritable, panicked, regressive, belligerent, people-pleasing, tearful, or dissociative when I am struggling.

Sometimes I feel shame about how my body chooses to show up while I am having a hard day. I judge myself and apologize constantly. I call myself "crazy" or "insane."

None of that is necessary.

I am a human being that is going through a tough time and trying to manage life with mental illness. I am not perfect, and that is okay.

I am not ashamed of how I show up when I am struggling.

The Darkness Part III

The further I make it in the healing process, the more acutely aware I am that "The Darkness" is not *me*.

It does not mean that I do not miss the darkness, and that I don't yearn for the familiarity of it at times…but I know now that it is not an integral part of who I spiritually am.

The darkness is what happened to me. It is not me.

Notes to self:

- Life should not be about simply surviving.

- Some days, self-care is a tiny revolt or simple pause before destructive behaviors.

- My struggle is mine and however it looks for me is valid.

- I am always healing, even on the difficult days.

- Vulnerability is hard, but silence is harder.

- Beneath comfort is change.

- Having hope is an act of bravery.

- Every season I am alive is a miracle.

- Life is happening **right now.**

The True Me

I want to be still, observing,
and contemplative when I please
I do not want to take up space
solely for entertainment purposes

I want all parts of me to be accepted
I do not want the expectation to always be happy,
friendly, excitable, or enthusiastic

I want to be able to maintain boundaries
after I set them
I do not want to feel like I owe everyone
every part of myself

I want to be able to tell men to leave if they
are bothering me or making me feel
uncomfortable
I do not want to be concerned with their opinion of
me or fall back into unhealthy patterns of
compliancy

I want to be able to show up exactly as I am
feeling in any given moment
I do not want to shift my behavior based on how
others respond to my big emotions

I want to put my own needs first
I do not want my needs to be confused with or
dependent upon the needs of others

I want to be able to protect myself and say
no
I do not want to say yes because I am afraid

Hey,
you.

Take your own advice.

Lovingly,
me.

Keep Walking Anyway

Strolling in the dark one spring evening, I can't tell if the stranger ahead on the sidewalk is walking towards me, or away from me. If they are moving forward, or backwards. They both appear the same without the brightness of the sun, the clear guidance of the light.

Life is like that sometimes. We do not know if the pain is progress, or if it is just meaningless suffering, pulling us back into the void. Sometimes it feels like we are walking in place, not moving at all. Like we are walking on an existential treadmill, with no end in sight.

The beauty is that we do not need to know the trajectory. It changes as quickly as day turns to night. It is a cycle we never master, and can be as unpredictable as the shifting of the seasons.

We keep walking anyway.

February 2nd, 2020

I have not sustained a prolonged period of starvation in over a year now. Being in recovery does not mean the horrible body image and thoughts of restriction go away, it means I have found something bigger than my disorder that allows me to ignore those thoughts and go about my day.

After my last relapse, I decided I can't live another day in the repetitive hell of anorexia, and I'm frankly just not ready to die yet. I was sick of forcing my body to sustain life on empty solely to avoid it. I remained curious and took things one day at a time.

Recovery has brought me so much more than being in small body did.

I think that is poetry all on its own.

I'm Not There Now

I told my therapist that I know I have made progress because now I fear death, when really it used to be all I thought about. All I welcomed. She expressed sadness at the thought of death by my own accord.

What a wonderfully strange feeling to be able to look her in the eye, smile, and truthfully say,

"You don't have to worry, I'm not there now."

Health Restored

Sometimes, things leave your life
uprooted
Sometimes, things reappear
unearthed
Never fear,
for it is all
in the name of growth

resiliency.

for

foundation

the

is

Ground zero

The human condition is to suffer,
yet we are granted a profound instinct
for survival

What a sick kind of beauty that is.

Recovery is finding things that feel like home, over and over, until you feel you truly are.

Home.

It is possible to practice gratitude and honor pain simultaneously. To be grateful is not to let the pain slip through the cracks. It is the most tender way to acknowledge your battles.

I am hurting, **and** *I am thankful for days where it doesn't hurt so much.*
I am struggling, **and** *I am grateful that I have survived until now.*
I am doubtful, **and** *I am glad that I continue to try.*

And…what a beautifully powerful word.

The beautiful thing
about tomorrow
is that you will always know
a little more
than you did today
and you can always be
a little better
than you were yesterday

-One Day Wiser

Two Choices

To make meaning
out of suffering
or to suffer
because of the meaning
we make

Healing is admission
to a world of consciousness
we never dreamed existed
What if we are all just here,
as the shortest moment of our lives
in this flesh on Earth
and we are actually supposed to live
infinitely among the stars and galaxy
after our bones turn to dust
We run through life saying,
This is it
this is the one life you have
But maybe,
this is just *one life* we have
among many others, too

What holds us back?
The lies our minds recycle
as familiar as old bedtime stories
Tales as old as time
Comfortable, maybe
Routine
But will never allow us
to sleep at night
like we would
if we placed our hands on our hearts
to guide us gently home

Imposters

The trauma became
a black hole,
lodging itself in my gut
leaving me chronically empty,
searching endlessly for ways
to fill this limitless void

Because of this
black hole in my gut,
I am lonely
I feel as though I do not
have a place in this world
Other people have happy lives
Other people find love,
have families,
or find fulfillment
and I am just…*here*
on the outside looking in
No one will ever understand
what it is like to live
in this body and this mind

My hope is that
there are thousands of us imposters
Beautifully imperfect misfits
who feel the exact the same way
and just because I cannot see
your black hole,
does not mean

it does not exist
In that sense,
I am not an *other*
I am one of many
And you are, too.

New Lease on Life
(Dear Reader)

Healing is not always what the poems say. It can be cruel.

When you are in the process of healing, you are the in-between. The in-between is having one foot in the shadows and the other in the unknown. You are far enough away from daily agony, yet haven't experienced the joy of being healed. You don't know what healed would even begin to look like.

Healing is the nitty gritty, dirt under your nails, sweat, blood, and tears hard work. It is deep breaths in the parking lot in the middle of your work day when you are triggered. It is nights in your car stalling because you are afraid of going inside and experiencing painful emotions. It is stuffing your sweatshirt in your mouth and screaming into the steering wheel after therapy. It is staring at the phone for two hours before finally calling for help.

Healing is at times, hopelessness. It feels like you are losing parts of yourself— the kind you don't want there, but don't know how to live without. Sometimes it feels more brutal than the original torment of survival. It is dramatic, but not in its speed. It is minor choices that lead to major ones. It is not walking, or even crawling. Some days it is stagnant, desperate, groveling. Sometimes it isn't gnawing the chain of depression off, it is simply being a compliant prisoner by staying alive. It is existence at its bare bones. It is baby bird fragility.

Day-to-day healing is not pretty. It is the slow march of continuing to scrape by. It is not being able to afford specialized therapy, but sacrificing in other areas because you have sacrificed your serenity for so long. It is profound loneliness, knowing you are walking this unseen journey separate from many others around you. Sometimes it is not joy, but merely the absence of fear. It is not big resolutions, but tiny boring habits you can commit to. It is not one day waking up and being magically better, rather, the pain lessening over time.

Sometimes the poems talk about healing in mystical and enchanting ways. It can be that certain days, sure…but to commit to true, long-lasting healing is to know and honor the awful. To respect and honor its sacredness, knowing that the gruesome times pave the road for the better times ahead.

2020

This year has been humbling for everyone, it seems. We have screamed. We have cried. We have waved triumphant middle fingers to the sky and cackled with absurdity. Our hearts have broken and our lungs weakened— the rise and fall of our chests our very own battle cries.

One day soon it will all make sense. Until then, we resist defeat and face each day as part of an infinite infantry...

for the war has only just begun.

We are the generation of healers.

We can end the cycle of trauma.

We can heal the wounds of insidious
silence;

of hurt people hurting people.

We can repair the damage that generations
of oppression has done.

We can raise the next generation to do the
same.

But we must do the work.

Knowing our behavioral patterns is fortune-telling. Our past selves hold the key.

Once we become conscious of these cycles, we are no longer afforded a life on autopilot.

We break again and again
only to heal ourselves.

Gaslighted

It was my fault
I deserve to be hurt
My problems are too much
Asking for help is weak
I scare people away
Nobody will ever love me

Imagine that the neuropathways in your brain are tire tracks in the mud. The more you drive over these tracks, the deeper they become. Your internal parts drive over them repeatedly, entertaining these harmful thoughts and taking actions that sanctify your agreement. Soon, the car starts to become stuck in the mud because of how deep the trenches are.

If you have had shameful or self-deprecating thoughts for as long as you can remember, your tracks are deep. Considering taking a different route is incomprehensible at times. These tracks are the veins of your entire existence. They are your lifeblood, your identity. To entertain the idea that you are worthy, that you are lovable, and that asking for help is okay, can feel like a threat to your entire system. A system so complex and engrained into every fiber of your being. A system you created *in order to survive.*

Do not blame yourself for feeling this way. Do not shame yourself by echoing other's wishes for you to "get over it" and get well. None of this is your fault. And just as easily as you can run a car back and forth to create deep lines in the dirt, you can grab someone you trust and let them help you fill some back in.

Thank you brain, for being creative in ways that helped me survive and cope for so many years, but I am going to try something different this time.

Now grab a shovel and get to work.

Love is the bravest thing
we will ever accomplish in life
We get married without knowing
we will be divorced years later
We have babies
that turn into adults
that turn into victims
that turn into monsters
We build homes we do not plan
to destroy one day
We love so deeply
we wonder which one of us
will die alone
Love is vulnerable.
Love is terrifying.
Love is courageous.

We, the People of Trauma

Every time we enter a new relationship, we open ourselves up to endless possibilities. It can be quite frightening at times. The fear usually does not stop many people in their pursuit of love. Fear is written in fine print, rather than bolded in the center of the page. It is present, but not the main attraction.

Then there is we, the people of trauma, who carry the burden of fear in a way that is crippling, isolating, and all-consuming at times. We want love and connection, yet are simultaneously terrified of reliving the pain again.

I hope you keep being brave enough to practice vulnerability and remain open to the possibility of love even after being hurt, if that is what you truly want in life.

And if you crave solitude, that is okay too.

You deserve someone
who loves you
for everything you are
not hate you,
for everything you are not
Who sees you
for who you are
not look past you,
for something better
Who appreciates you
for who you will grow into
not resent you,
for becoming someone new

I Loved You Once

Everyone in your life now will not stay. Some will teach you lessons you did not ask for. Some will show you what you need to heal.

I did not know my ex-husband was a lesson. I did not know he would help me learn what I would not tolerate. I did not know he would teach me how to leave.

I did not know some friends were frauds. I did not know they would help me learn how to be angry for my younger self. I did not know they would teach me that softness is not a curse.

I did not know some relationships were temporary. I did not know they would help me learn to love and then let go.

The older I become, the more I realize that not everyone is meant to stay. People change, and so do we. That is the beauty of life, of the seasons, of the rotation of the Earth itself. I try to accept the new lessons I will be taught, even when they are painful. It is a muscle I build stronger over time.

I loved you once, I don't anymore, and now it is time to let you go.

How tragic it is,
that we continually punish ourselves for
what others have done to us

It is the most twisted form of retribution
that exists

Love is not supposed to hurt.
Love is not supposed to hurt.
Love is not supposed to hurt.
Love is not supposed to hurt.
Love is not supposed to hurt.
Love is not supposed to hurt.
Love is not supposed to hurt.
Love is not supposed to hurt.
Love is not supposed to hurt.
Love is not supposed to hurt.
Love is not supposed to hurt.
Love is not supposed to hurt.
Love is not supposed to hurt.
Love is not supposed to hurt.
Love is not supposed to hurt.
Love is not supposed to hurt.
Love is not supposed to hurt.
Love is not supposed to hurt.
Love is not supposed to hurt.
Love is not supposed to hurt.
Love is not supposed to hurt.
Love is not supposed to hurt.
Love is not supposed to hurt.
Love is not supposed to hurt.
Love is not supposed to hurt.
Love is not supposed to hurt.
Love is not supposed to hurt.
Love is not supposed to hurt.
Love is not supposed to hurt.
Love is not supposed to hurt.
Love is not supposed to hurt

I

Throughout my life, I consistently found comfort in the façade of *"I'm fine."* My parents, friends, and even therapists would tell me how well I appeared to handling things. By the time I reached crisis mode, people around me were shocked and surprised. *"I had no idea you were struggling,"* they'd say.

If you are that person to the rest of your loved ones, *I see you.* I know how hard it can be. You deserve to have your fragility acknowledged, too. Compulsive self-reliance is not a ticket to "strong." Isolation is not the price we have to pay to be alive.

It is okay to not always be the tough one.

II

If you are a highly sensitive person, I hope you understand just how beautiful you are. We need more of you in this world, not less. It can feel like a curse to feel so much, but it is also a blessing because it softens us to other people's struggles.

We are the ones who have the capacity to truly make a difference in this world.

What a gift that is.

III

Being on the deep, dark path to healing can be lonely at times. Not everyone is interested in bettering themselves, and many people are uninterested, not ready, or simply don't know where to begin.

Even if you may feel alone, even if you physically are alone in this moment... spiritually you are not. An invisible thread connects all of us who have been through similar pain.

Never stop trying to find the people who understand.

On Truth-Telling

Some people may resent you for speaking up— these are the ones you are holding the mirror up to, forcing to face themselves. These are the people that need to hear it the most.

Some may not understand why you are speaking up— these are the ones you have an opportunity to educate, that can bring about change.

Some may be entirely supportive and loving— these are the ones you hold close to your heart, that you ask to walk beside you on your road to healing.

You never know who you may be helping by using your voice.

[Even if that person is you].

On Expectations

Healing comes when we release expectations of how others should treat us when we are in pain.

If you have a history of relational trauma, you may be sensitive to tone of voice, body language cues, and perceived invalidation. It can make reaching out difficult at times because we cannot control people's reactions or words towards us. One "wrong" move could be the difference between our trauma being triggered and us never wanting to reach out again.

As we grow wiser, we must remind ourselves often that the people we interact with (including professionals), are human and filtering their words through their own experiences. There is no such thing as a perfect reaction. At the same time, we should keep trying to find people who continually hold space for our feelings, rather than try to fix it or make it about themselves.

It is a fine balance that we are granted permission to work on with each passing day. Keep pushing yourself to reach out. Corrective experiences with a trusted person can heal the soul from the inside, out.

The Fridge

Trauma extends into every facet of our lives. It affects how and when we ask for help, what we deem worthy of trying to fix, and the amount of pain we are willing to carry.

I live in an apartment with an older fridge. At some point, my fridge started leaking water from the plastic surrounding the lightbulb. It would drip onto my lower shelf, then freeze. Raising the temperature of the fridge made the lightbulb area drip more. Lowering the temperature would freeze all my food.

For an entire year, I chipped ice off my bottom shelf. I put jugs underneath the lightbulb area to catch the drips and emptied it when it froze. I threw out countless cans of exploded sodas. I stopped buying lettuce because it would freeze and go to waste. I simply thought, *Oh, this is how it is now.* I just don't eat salads anymore.

Not once did I think to tell my landlord about the issue. It never even crossed my mind that someone else could help me find a solution to it.

Living through seemingly unlivable events changes the parts of our brain that help us problem-solve. It changes our survival instincts. It makes the amount of pain (or in this case, inconvenience), we can tolerate extremely high at times.

After months of therapy, I marched into the leasing office with confidence one day and told them my problem. They ordered a new fridge that day. I didn't realize that what I was tolerating was unnecessary until my landlord said to me, "You shouldn't have to live like that, throwing away all your food!" She had a strange look on her face when I told her how long I had waited. The proverbial light bulb turned on. And just like that, my problem was solved.

A lot of us live our lives with broken fridges, when there is a repair man right around the corner. You may have done things on your own for a while now, and that is an accomplishment to be proud of, but please know there are people who can and are willing to help.

If you simply ask.

Am I Healing?

If you are asking yourself this question, you already know the answer.

Keep going.

Future Us

In recovery, we are told to cherish and appreciate our younger selves for doing whatever it took to survive. We are taught to forgive them and show them kindness.

Our future selves deserve love too! For who they are, and who they will become. Take actions now that your future self would be proud of. Dream of how courageous and brilliant they will be. Their resilience is contingent on who you are and what you are doing right in this moment.

Russian Roulette

In my 20's, I thought I could outrun my pain until it was no longer relevant. I thought I would "grow up" and not think about the past anymore. I shelved the memories for later while I busied myself with various addictions: workaholism, eating disorders, self-harm, alcoholism, perfectionism, and obsessive-compulsive behaviors.

The pain did not go away. It remained dormant, sometimes faded or forgotten over time. But time does not heal all wounds.

I grew older physically, but mentally I became stuck. Soon life became a race of which came first: my demise or my remedy. Every time I hit "rock bottom," I tried my hardest to get well, until I realized I could (and would) eventually dig deeper.

I could not engage in behaviors casually anymore. My half-hearted attempts at avoidance soon became a panicked desperation; a rush to outrun the wave of emotions and memories. I knew someday I would crash and burn, but I fought the pain until the very last second I was able to. I was not just *choosing* to engage in unhealthy coping mechanisms anymore. They became a part of me and my brain chemistry. I could not function with or without them. I played Russian Roulette with these behaviors over and over. Stop over-exercising, start drinking. Get sober, self-harm. The game of destroying myself never ceased.

If you relate to any of this, I offer this from a deep place of knowing: I hope you scare yourself enough to get well. Because choosing to get well and staying well are two very different things. I know how hard it is to want to stop these behaviors, while simultaneously feeling powerless against them.

Trauma is not reasonable. It is not linear. It is not systematic or categorical. There comes a time when the burden will become so heavy, that healing will become your number one priority and full-time job. It is that, or death. Spiritual, physical, or both. Healing becomes the be all, end all. I hope that time comes for you. Not because I want you to hurt yourself, but because it is a relief and an unburdening to simply know within your heart that *it is not an option anymore.*

To have this type of brazenness is the desperation we all need in our lives— to do whatever it takes to get well, no matter the circumstances.

Be well.

Day 183
[Without You]

I wish I could offer some supreme wisdom on how to heal from things like this, but I'm not there yet. I'm now living in a modest apartment, licking my wounds and attempting to maintain some semblance of routine and balance in my life. My hope is that one day I will be able to look back on this and see it as a blessing. For now, I am engaging in copious amounts of distraction and simply swallowing the grief in small doses.

This life is lonely much of the time, but keeping my head pointed in the direction of continued growth is how I survive. The unknowns are pretty scary, but the possibilities keep me curious enough to hold on just a little longer.

So This is Healing

Drag me slowly
across gravel roads
with bloodied knees
and dirt between my teeth
I am spitting poison
the kind that marinates in your bones
ravaged by an illness
only my trauma knows, because
Life is insidious
you die slowly to stay alive
and healing is
the medicine that burns

Break my ankles
so that I am constantly on my knees
I pray to a God I do not know
saying I will be good, please
I am tending wounds
the kind you nor I can see
Bargaining to the heavens
just take this pain away, because
Life is winter's sting
reminding you of injuries you used to know
and healing is
an army crawl to spring

Drown me tenderly
tying weights to my feet
watch me try to swim

but I never really sink
I am gasping for air
the kind that is never enough
Waters I've known so long
I hold my breath, because
Life is underwater
your lungs submerged for years
And healing is
learning how to breathe again

Modalities that I have found helpful on my
treatment/therapy journey:

Internal Family Systems Therapy [IFS]:
https://ifs-institute.com/

**Eye Movement Rapid Desensitization
Therapy [EMDR]:**
https://www.emdr.com/

Somatic Experiencing:
https://www.somaticexperiencing.com/

Brainspotting:
https://brainspotting.com/

Stellate-Ganglion Block for PTSD:
https://stellacenter.com/treatment/

Acknowledgements

I want to thank some special people who have been a part of my journey these past few years.

Mom & Dad- for continuing to be present with me through the ups and downs of having a child with mental illness, even through worry and fear. Even when you do not understand my struggle, you never stop trying to educate yourselves and be a part of the conversation. You let me ask for what I need to stay well and always try to support in any way you can. You have grown with me and have done your own internal work as well.

Jennifer- for refusing to give up on me, for being patient and loving with me through the hard weeks (and the really, really hard weeks), for continually reminding me that I am not alone, and for inspiring many poems throughout this book. You listen to me with love and nonjudgment and make reaching out a safe option always. It is one of the most beautiful gifts I have ever been given.

Tara- for reminding me that my body holds important wisdom, for graciously offering advice and unwavering support throughout the years, for seeing the true me, and for inspiring many poems in *bare roots*. You continue to be a safe person for me through struggle and growth, and that is so special.

Annika- for bringing stability and peace throughout my divorce, for being brave enough to approach the hard discussions about my eating disorder, and for empathy in a time of crisis. You let me have my own journey and always reminded me that you were there to support. I am thankful for your light in a time when I felt only darkness.

Treatment in 2018 (Center names redacted)- For staff that tried to understand the struggle, and for the patients who knew what it was like: I could not have recovered without your patience and camaraderie. Many days I was brave because you all were, too. Your hugs and laughter helped me survive the most harrowing of days.

To my friends, online and in the recovery community- thank you for being a safe haven for me to vent to when I felt misunderstood and alone. Thank you for witnessing the highs and lows and standing by me, even though some of you have never even met me in person.

To my friends, who know me in present life- for reminding me I am loved for who I am, for continuing to stay in touch even when I try to disappear, and for checking in on me because you care.

To my readers- I would not feel brave enough to keep writing if you all had not been such a brilliant pillar of positivity and support after the release of my first book, and I continue to be brave because you all are, too. If this is your first experience reading work of mine, thank you for being willing to go there with me. Please never stop searching for something better and reaching out to me if you feel compelled. You are not alone.

I am so grateful to have met so many beautiful souls along my journey.